I love food! It fills my tummy from breakfast to bedtime.

**Breakfast**

Food looks good. It smells good.

Sweet or sour, salty and spicy,
I love it all!

Food is fun. At breakfast, Mum goes "crunch!" on her toast.

I make a face in my porridge. The honey and raisins make it sweet.

**Porridge**

Dad's grapefruit looks good, so I try a bit. Ooh! That tastes sour!

"Can I add some honey?" I ask.

Eating a grapefruit

Today I am going on a picnic. So after breakfast, we go to the shops.

We buy fruit and vegetables. Those apples look good!

**Fruit**

"Do you want to bake biscuits for the picnic?" asks Mum.

"Yes, please," I say. So we buy eggs, butter, flour and sugar.

When we get home, I help Mum to make the dough. We mix the eggs, butter, flour and sugar.

Flour

Sugar

Eggs

Butter

Then my friends Greg and Susan come to play.

They help us to make biscuits.

**Making biscuits**

We roll the dough flat and cut out lots of shapes.

"They look good!" says Mum. Then she puts them in the oven.

Biscuit dough

Then we make ham, lettuce and tomato sandwiches.

"They look good," says Mum. "Let's take some apples and bananas, too."

**Making sandwiches**

**Bread**

**Apple**

**Lettuce**

**Tomatoes**

**Banana**

"Something smells good!" I say.

"The biscuits are done," says Mum.
"But hands off until the picnic!"

Lots of friends come to the picnic.
They all bring things to eat.

Fruit

Prawn crackers

Spicy
foods

Pitta
bread

Look at all the food!

I feel hungry already!

Drinks

Sandwiches

Salty snacks

Vegetables

Pizza

First we play catch with a ball.
Soon we are very hungry.

We sit down on the rug. "Food is
fun to eat outside," says Susan.

**Playing catch**

There is lots of food to eat.
Everyone loves our biscuits!

After the picnic, we run and
play all afternoon.

**Eating the picnic**

When we get home,
Dad is making a chilli.

He puts in beef, beans, onions,
a pinch of salt and some spices.

Adding spices

"Hot spices make your mouth feel like fire," says Dad.

"But a little spice can make food taste good."

Chilli

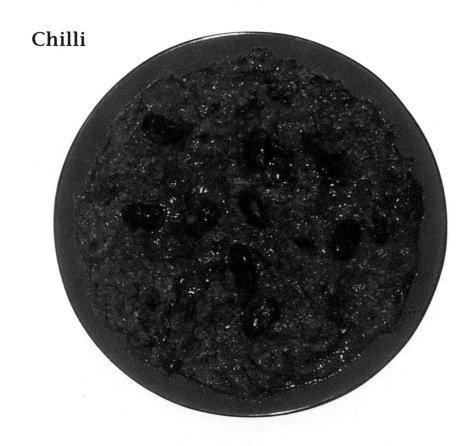

Soon the chilli is ready.
We sit down for dinner.

"That looks good,"
says Mum.

"It smells good,"
I say.

"Does it
taste good?"
asks Dad.

"It tastes great!"
I say.

Sweet or sour, salty and spicy,
I love food!

Dinner

Here are some words and phrases from the book.

Picnic

Making biscuits

Lettuce

Eat a grapefruit

Bowl of chilli

Breakfast

Make sandwiches

Add spices

Can you use these words to write your own story?

# Did you see these in the book?

### Pineapple

### Tangerines

### Apples

### Rolling pin

© Aladdin Books Ltd 2001
All rights reserved
Designed and produced by
Aladdin Books Ltd
28 Percy Street
London W1T 2BZ
Literacy Consultant
Phil Whitehead
Printed in U.A.E.

First published in
Great Britain in 2001 by
Franklin Watts
96 Leonard Street
London EC2A 4XD

A catalogue record for this
book is available from the
British Library.

ISBN 0 7496 4842 2

Illustrator
Mary Lonsdale - SGA
Picture Credits
All photos by Select
Pictures except 10-11, 24br
– Becky Luigart-Stayner
/CORBIS.